Clothes & Uniforms

Kath Cox and Pat Hughes

Wayland

Notes for Parents and Teachers

This book provides a flexible teaching resource for Early Years History. Two levels of text are given – a simple version and a more advanced and extended version. The book can be used for:

♦ Early stage readers at Key Stage 1
♦ Older readers needing differentiated text
♦ Non-readers who can use the photographs
♦ Extending skills of reading non-fiction
♦ Adults reading aloud to provide a model for non-fiction reading

By comparing photographs from the past and the present, children are able to develop skills of observation, ask questions and discuss ideas. They should begin by identifying the familiar in the modern photographs before moving on to the photographs from the past. The aim is to encourage children to make 'now' and 'then' comparisons.

The use of old photographs not only provides an exciting primary resource for History but, used alongside the modern photographs, aids the discussion of the development of photography. Modern photographs in black and white are included to encourage children to look more closely at the photographs and avoid seeing the past as 'black and white'. All the historical photographs were taken beyond the living memory of children and most have been selected from the Edwardian period between 1900–1920.
A comprehensive information section for teachers, parents and other adults on pages 29–31 gives details of each of the old photographs, where known, and suggests points to explore and questions to ask children.

Editor: Carron Brown
Designer: Michael Leaman
Production Controller: Carol Stevens
Consultant: Norah Granger

Front cover: The main picture features two boys sailor suits and a girl, 1900s.
Endpapers: Photographers at work at a wedding, 1907.
Title page: Firemen on a Merryweather fire engine, 1903.

Picture Acknowledgements
The publishers would like to thank the following for allowing their pictures to be used in this book: Danny Allmark 14; Bolton Museum and Art Gallery 13; Duncan H. W. Brown 6; Chapel Studios 10; Mary Evans Picture Library *title page*, 19, 23; Eye Ubiquitous 8, 20; Glasgow University Archives *cover* (main) 7, 11; Sally and Richard Greenhill 4; Robert Harding 16; Hulton Getty 5, 9, 15, 25; Norfolk Libraries 17; Royal Photographic Society *contents page*; Stickphotos (Trevor Wood) 12; Tony Stone *cover* (inset); Topham Picture Source 18, 21, 26; Wayland Picture Library 22, 24, /Imperial War Museum 27.

First published in 1996 by Wayland Publishers Limited
61 Western Road, Hove, East Sussex BN3 1JD, England

© Copyright 1996 Wayland Publishers Limited

The right of Kath Cox and Pat Hughes to be identified as the authors of this work has been asserted in accordance with the Copyright, Designs and Patents Act 1988.

British Library Cataloguing in Publication Data
Cox, Kathleen
Clothes and Uniforms. – (History from Photographs)
1. Costume – Great Britain – History – Juvenile literature
2. Uniforms – Great Britain – History – Juvenile literature
I. Title II. Hughes, Pat, 1933 – 391.00941

ISBN 0-7502-1544-5

Typeset in the UK by Michael Leaman Design Partnership
Printed and bound in Great Britain by B.P.C. Paulton Books Ltd

ᐧ Contents ᐧ

A Brownie box camera and case, 1900.

Mrs Benn is holding her baby.

It is Daniel's
christening day.
He is wearing a
long, white dress
bought specially
for him.
Daniel has a vest
and disposable
nappy under his
dress.

Most baby clothes were made of wool or cotton.

It took a long time to wash and dry baby clothes.
Cloth nappies were washed and worn again.
Babies from rich families had many clothes.
In poor families, babies were often wrapped in rags.

Rory is going for a walk.

He is wearing a coat called an anorak.
It is easy to put on and take off because it fastens with a zip.
Rory's anorak is made from material that is light but very warm and comfortable.
It can be washed and dried quickly.

This little girl wore
a coat too.

Coats were made of heavy
materials and fastened with
buttons or ribbons.
Most children wore bonnets or hats.
Children wore several layers of clothing to keep warm.

This is the de Souza family.

They are all wearing comfortable clothes, and trainers or shoes.
These are made of materials that are brightly coloured,
hard-wearing and easy to clean.
Modern homes are warm so people do not need to wear many layers
of clothing when they are inside.

This family wore smart clothes.

Women wore long skirts but not trousers.

Men wore suits and shirts with stiff collars.

Boys wore dresses until they were three years old when they got their first pair of trousers.

Edwardian homes were cold and people had to wear many layers of clothing.

The Wood family like to go walking.

They are wearing clothes that keep them warm and dry.
Scott and Robert use their hoods to keep out the wind.
Hiking boots and trainers are comfortable for walking long distances.

People dressed smartly to go for a walk.

Adults and children usually wore hats.

Women liked large hats with wide brims.

Ribbons and flowers were used to decorate the hats.

Some men wore hats like the one in the picture.

It is called a Homburg hat.

Other men wore bowler hats or flat caps.

These children are wearing different types of clothes.

Most parents buy their children's clothes in shops.

Few children wear home-made clothes.

Shops sell many styles of clothing for children.

Children often wear special clothes for different activities such as playing sport.

Children all wore the same kinds of clothes.

Clothes were often passed on to younger children.

Girls wore woollen dresses with pinafores on top.

Sometimes, they also wore shawls to keep them warm.

Boys wore woollen jackets and trousers.

Some people wore clogs instead of boots or shoes.

This is a photograph of Jill and Ray on their wedding day.

Jill, the bride, chose her white dress from a special shop.

The bridesmaids are wearing dresses that have been made for them.

Ray, the groom, is wearing his best suit.

Their family and friends are all wearing smart clothes.

Only rich families would have a wedding like this.

Men wore suits with waistcoats and top hats.

Brides wore cream or white dresses and carried flowers.

The dresses of the bride, bridesmaids and guests were made by a seamstress.

Brides from poorer families were usually married wearing their best dresses.

It is a hot day and the beach is busy.

People are sunbathing and paddling in the sea.
Most of them are wearing beach clothes.
The men are wearing swimming trunks and women are wearing
bikinis or swimming costumes.
People put sun-tan lotion on their skin to stop it getting burnt
in the hot sun.

This beach was busy too.

People wore their ordinary clothes when they went to the seaside.
They did not want to get a sun tan so they kept their skin covered with their clothes.
Many people thought it was wrong to show their bare arms and legs.

Footballers wear uniforms, called strips.

The men are wearing shirts, shorts and socks in the team colours.

Football shirts usually have a logo on the front.

The player's name and number are on the back.

Footballers wear shin-pads under their socks to protect their legs.

Football kits are made of light, comfortable material.

Football teams had their own strips.

Footballers wore plain, woollen shirts and long, cotton shorts.
These kits were not easy to wash and keep clean.
Football boots were made of leather with studs on the soles.
Dubbin was rubbed into the leather to keep the boots soft and waterproof.

Amy works in McDonalds.

All the staff wear the
same style of uniform.
Men and women wear
striped shirts and blue
trousers.
The hat has a logo
on the front.
The company wants its
staff to look smart.

These ladies wore a uniform for their work.

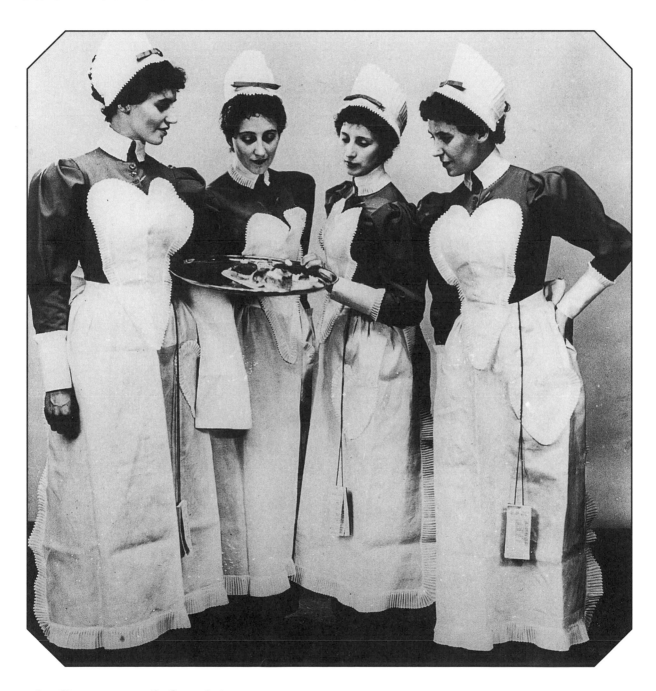

These ladies served food in a restaurant.

Waitresses wore long, white aprons over their dresses to keep them clean.

Collars, cuffs and caps were dipped in starch to make them stiff.

Most police officers wear uniforms.

Men wear dark-blue jackets, trousers, ties and white shirts.

Women wear dark-blue jackets, and skirts or trousers.

Badges and stripes show the officers' ranks.

Today, police officers wear hats with peaks.

Some police officers who do special jobs wear different uniforms.

Only men were police officers.

Police officers wore long, woollen coats with leather belts and silver buttons.
A whistle was fastened to a chain at the front of each coat.
The helmet was held on by a strap under the chin.
These helmets were hard and heavy but they protected the police officers' heads.
Policemen needed to wear comfortable leather boots.

These people work in a hospital.

The doctor is wearing a clean white coat over her ordinary clothes.
The other people are all nurses.
Nurses wear different uniforms depending on their job.
For example, doctors and nurses who help with operations usually wear green trousers, jackets and caps. They wear a new, clean uniform for each operation.

All nurses wore the same type of uniform.

Nurses in different hospitals often wore dresses of different colours.
The dresses were protected by white aprons that could be easily washed.
White cuffs helped to keep the long sleeves of the dresses clean.
Nurses put on red capes when they went outside the hospital.

Chris is a soldier.

This is his combat, or fighting, uniform.

The material is cool and light but very strong.

The jacket and trousers have many pockets to hold equipment.

Chris is wearing a hat called a beret.

The badge on his beret shows the name of his regiment.

These soldiers were going to fight.

They wore heavy khaki uniforms that helped to camouflage them.
Round metal helmets protected the soldiers' heads.
Strips of cloth called puttees were wound round the soldiers' legs.
Soldiers carried their equipment in pouches or strapped to their belts.

· Picture Glossary ·

 **Apron** Clothing that is worn over normal clothes to keep them clean, and tied at the back with strings.

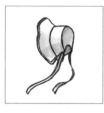 **Bonnet** A woman's or child's hat that covers the head and fastens under chin with strings or ribbons.

 **Bowler hat** A man's hat with a round top and a brim all round.

 **Clogs** Shoes that are made of leather and wood.

 **Dubbin** A type of grease put on leather to keep it soft and waterproof.

 **Puttee** A long, narrow strip of cloth worn round the leg from the ankle to the knee.

 **Seamstress** A woman who makes clothes from patterns and material.

 **Shawl** A piece of material worn round the shoulders, worn by women and girls.

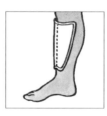 **Shin-pads** These are made of plastic and cloth. People who play football or hockey wear them at the front of their legs to protect them.

 **Suit** A jacket and trousers or skirt made from the same material.

 **Trainer** A sports shoe usually made from leather with rubber soles.

 **Waistcoat** A garment with no sleeves. It fastens at the front and is usually worn under a jacket.

·Books to Read·

Clothes by K. Bryant-Mole (History from Objects series, Wayland, 1994).
Clothes by R. Thomson (Changing Times series, Franklin Watts, 1992).
Getting Dressed by S. Jackson & T. Wood. (Turn of the Century series,
    A & C Black, 1992).
People Who Help Us by K. Cox & P. Hughes. (History From Photographs series,
    Wayland, 1995).
What We Wore by S. Ross (Starting History Series, Wayland, 1991).
When I was Young by R. Thomson (Early 20th Century series, Franklin Watts, 1993).

·Places to Visit·

Many local museums have small collections or displays of clothing, accessories or uniforms. It is worth contacting them to see what they can offer. In some areas there are small museums linked to branches of the armed forces, police or fire services with displays. The following examples are specialist costume museums.

Bexhill Manor Costume Museum
Manor House Gardens
Old Town
Bexhill-on-Sea
East Sussex TN40 2JA

   Telephone: 01424 215361

The Museum of Costume and Textiles
43-51 Castle Gate
Nottingham NG1 6AF

   Telephone: 01602 411881

Shambellie House Museum of Costume
New Abbey, Nr. Dumfries
Dumfriesshire

   Telephone: 0138 785375

The Gallery of English Costume
Platt Hall, Platt Fields
Rusholme
Manchester M14 5LL

   Telephone: 0161 224 5217

The Museum of Costume
Assembly Rooms
Bennett St, Bath
Avon BA1 2QH

   Telephone: 01225 461111

Further Information about the Photographs

Mrs MacNaughton and her baby, 13 July 1903.

About this photograph

Babies in rich families had many clothes. A soft muslin square was placed next to the baby's skin under a towelling nappy fastened with a safety pin. At night a flannel pilch was added to help absorption. A strip of material was often wound round the baby's back to add support. Several layers of clothing would be worn depending on the season. A baby would usually wear a woollen vest, drawers, a long dress and a woollen jacket. Bootees covered the feet. Working-class babies would be clothed in home-sewn and second-hand clothes.

Questions to ask

Is this a special occasion? How can you tell?
Is the baby a boy or a girl?
How is the baby's robe decorated?

Points to explore

Compare materials available for baby clothes then and now.
Investigate ceremonies associated with the birth or naming of a baby.

Miss Daisy Jackson, March 1913.

About this photograph

This little girl is dressed in a very fashionable outfit of the time. Pastel colours, large collars and decorative embroidery were fashionable. Children, like adults, wore hats for most occasions. Woollen stockings, mittens and leather-bar shoes completed the outfit. Several layers of heavy material restricted freedom of movement. Boys were dressed like girls until the age of three or four.

Questions to ask

How are the clothes decorated? Do the clothes look comfortable?
Would the clothes be easy to keep clean?

Points to explore

Look at clothes worn by children in other photographs from the time.
Compare fastenings, i.e. buttons, to what is available today.

Family group, 1900.

About this photograph

In late Victorian and early Edwardian times, women wore high-necked blouses, puffed sleeves and belts that accentuated small waists restricted by corsets. The tailored 'costume' comprised of a short jacket, a long, full skirt and blouse or waistcoat. Men's fashion changed less rapidly. Boys wore dresses until their third birthday when they were 'breeched' (given their first pair of trousers). Older boys often wore tweed suits with knickerbocker trousers. Girls wore dark woollen or serge dresses, black woollen stockings and button boots.

Questions to ask

Who are the people in the photograph?
What is the little boy wearing? How are the clothes decorated?

Points to explore

Use information books to name the different garments seen.
Collect modern clothes. Label them with names and materials.

Walking at Archerfield, East Lothian, August 1911.

About this photograph

Clothes for the middle class were formal, even on informal occasions such as a walk. Hats were worn outside. Women's hats were large, wide-brimmed, heavily trimmed with feathers, flowers and ribbons and secured with long hatpins. Men wore Homburg hats made of felt, velure or straw. The gentleman wears a high, stiff collar that dug into the neck. The woman in the centre wears an outfit that reflects the less-restricting styles seen from 1910 onwards. Young girls wore their hair loose or with ribbons. Girls and women never wore trousers.

Questions to ask

Why is everyone wearing hats? What are the two old ladies carrying?
Would these clothes be comfortable to walk in?
What were some of the problems with long skirts?

Points to explore

Compare these clothes to those of workers in the country at that time.
Investigate the various outdoor clothes worn for walking today.

Children at Election time, Farnworth near Bolton, c.1900.

About this photograph

Children wore hand-me-downs or second-hand clothes that would be repeatedly repaired. Some families paid a penny a week to a clothing club to buy clothes and shoes for their children. Most girls wore plain, loose woollen dresses. Starched-white pinafores were worn on top of the dresses to protect them. Hats were worn for best wear, even in the poorest families. Boys wore miniature versions of clothes worn by adults. Clogs were worn by adults and children in many areas. Clogs were a cheaper alternative to boots and shoes. They were strong, weather-proof and insulated the foot against the cold.

Questions to ask

What different types of headgear can be seen?
What were the advantages of clogs?

Points to explore

Compare clothes of poor and wealthy children using old photographs.
Look at the variety of children's clothes available today.

Wedding group, 1910.

About this photograph

Only a wealthy family could afford these wedding clothes. The bride would wear a long dress of cream or white crepe de Chine, taffeta or satin with embroidery, ruffles and lace decoration. This would be dyed or re-styled for further wear. On formal occasions, gentlemen wore long frock coats and stiff wing collars with top hats. The bearded man is dressed in a mid-Victorian style. A working-class bride would wear her best dress or make a dress that could be worn again.

Questions to ask

Which lady is the bride? How can you tell?
What colours might the clothes be?

Points to explore

Similarities with modern formal weddings.
Find about wedding clothes from different cultures.

Gorleston-on-Sea, Norfolk, 1908.

About this photograph

The only allowance made for the location and heat is the removal of boots and stockings by children, and boys rolling up their trouser legs. Tanned skin was considered undesirable as it suggested rough country life. The late Victorian swimming outfit for women comprised of a navy blue serge costume with a long skirt over baggy calf-length legs and decorated with frills and braid. From 1900 a one piece costume made of lighter weight stockinette was available. Men wore a one piece bathing suit that covered the torso and part of the legs.

Questions to ask

Why did people wear so many clothes in hot weather and at the seaside?

What would it feel like to wear a suit or long dress on a hot day?

Points to explore

Discuss the ways in which we protect ourselves from the sun.

Look at clothing worn for other leisure pursuits in Edwardian times.

Woolich Arsenal football team, 1908–1909.

About this photograph

In 1863, Association Football was founded. The kits worn revealed very little of the body. High-necked, long-sleeved jeseys were worn with knee-length, baggy cotton shorts. No badges or logos were visible. Woollen socks and lace-up leather boots completed the kit. The goalkeeper wore a flat cap and his jersey had a cotton collar.

Questions to ask

Why was the photograph taken?

What is the older man carrying over his shoulder? Why?

What colours might the footballers' shirts be?

Points to explore

Look at other old photographs showing sports clothes or uniforms.

Compare their uniforms with todays wide range sports clothes.

Waitresses known as Nippys, 1920s.

About this photograph

'Nippys' were waitresses who worked in the many Lyons corner houses, teashops and restaurants. The name was given to them in 1909 and reflected the need to serve large numbers of customers quickly and efficiently. The uniform was very strict. Make-up had be inconspicuous and teeth well-cared for. Hair had to be neat and tidy, and hands well-manicured. The white collars, cuffs and aprons had to be clean and well-laundered. Only plain black stockings were permitted, and shoes had to be medium-heeled and well-polished. Caps had to be placed at the correct angle on their heads.

Questions to ask

Why are the waitresses wearing hats?

What problems would these uniforms cause for the wearer?

What is hanging on the end of the string? How would this be used?

Points to explore

Compare the Edwardian uniforms to waitress uniforms today.

Police officers in Wales during the coal strike, 1910.

About this photograph

Policemen wore the same basic uniform. Chevrons on the coat sleeves distinguished one rank from another. An armlet was placed on the sleeve when an officer was on duty. From 1864, helmets were the standard headgear, worn to protect the wearer. A badge on the front bore the division letter and number. Walking the beat made strong and comfortable boots a necessity. The whistle replaced the wooden rattle as the method of summoning help.

Questions to ask

Why are the police officers wearing helmets?

What is on the helmets? Why is it important?

What are some of the policemen holding in their hands?

What colour was their uniform?

Points to explore

Compare the technology and equipment available to policemen on the beat in 1900 and police officers today. Use photographs showing policemen in Edwardian times to find out what type of work they did.

Nurses, July 1913.

About this photograph

The basic nursing uniform consisted of an ankle-length, long-sleeved dress with a white apron, collar and cuffs. In some hospitals, skirts had trains so that the nurses' legs would be covered when a nurse leant over a bed. A cap was worn. Matrons wore black. From 1914, skirts got a little shorter and the uniform began to be more practical.

Questions to ask

What does the cross on the aprons represent?

What is the lady on the left wearing on her dress?

Points to explore

Investigate modern nursing uniforms (male and female, different colours worn by different ranks, different types of nurses).

British soldiers off to war, c. 1914.

About this photograph

In 1902, the khaki uniform became standard service issue. Trousers and jackets were made of serge, which was difficult to wash. Woollen coats were worn in cold weather. Puttees protected the trousers from dirt and the legs from minor injury. Helmets were made of steel and often covered with sacking. Leather boots completed the uniform. Soldiers wore a webbing harness with wide braces. Leather packs and pouches were buckled on to this webbing to hold equipment. Other items were carried in haversacks or strung across the body.

Questions to ask

What else do they have to carry with them? Why?

What colours do you think the uniforms are? Why were they chosen?

Points to explore

Use information books to find out about the different types of uniforms worn by the modern army (e.g. parade, arctic, desert). Collect other photographs of soldiers from the time and note similarities and differences in their uniforms.

·Index·

(Items that appear in text)

32